A Student's Guide to

The Longest Memory

by Fred D'Aguiar

Susan Perry
B.A., Dip.Ed., Dip. Social Sciences

First published in 1997 by
Wizard Books Pty Ltd
ACN 054 644 361
P.O. Box 304 Ballarat 3353 Australia
Email: wizard@netconnect.com.au
Reprinted 2000

ISBN 1 875739 63 7

Cover design by Cressaid Media
Cover art by Jon Crawley

Printed by Sands Print Group, Perth

Wizard Books gratefully acknowledges the permission of Random House (UK) for permission to reproduce quotations from *The Longest Memory* ©Fred D'Aguiar 1994

Contents

NOTES ON THE AUTHOR

Fred D'Aguiar was born in London on 2 February, 1960. His parents were from British Guyana (South America), where he spent most of his childhood. He returned to England at the age of twelve. He obtained a Bachelor of Arts with honours from the University of Kent at Canterbury in 1985. He went on to become a university teacher, specialising in poetry. He has been working since 1992 at American universities.

He is the author of three books of poetry, *Mama Dot* (1985), *Airy Hall* (1989), and *British Subjects* (1993). The first two recall his youth in Guyana, using Creole within the poems, while the latter looks at contemporary England.

Recognised internationally as a significant poet, D'Aguiar has won the T.S. Eliot Prize and the Guyana Prize for Poetry. He has also written one play, *A Jamaican Airman Foresees his Death* (1995), and two novels.

The Longest Memory came out of D'Aguiar's awareness of the way the crimes of the past weigh even today on people of African descent.

> Young blacks my age...people from the street who didn't even care about writing, articulated their rage about that past. And a lot of their relationships in the present seemed to be governed by this history. People won't let them forget it. You are still a nigger or a wog just because an ancestor was once owned by someone....So I thought one way of looking at the present and trying to make sense of it would be to actually come through the past....I was interested when I got to America where slavery had lived and breathed in the soil, to set the book there....I thought, give [the story] a plantation, a house, a solid institution and see how people move in that geography, in that space. ((Mary-Ann Metcalf's interview with the author, *Random House Australia*)

The novel was published in 1994, to great critical acclaim (see Critics below), immediately winning England's two most prestigious awards for a first novel: the Whitbread First Novel Award and the David Higham First Novel Award. It was on the list of Best Books for Young Adults 1996, compiled by the Young Adult Library Services Association (YALSA), a division of the American Library Association.

D'Aguiar's most recent novel, *Dear Future*, is the story of a Guyanese family, set against an impending election and an act of violence. It explores the way stories of the past and present are constructed.

He says about his writing:

> My poetry and prose deal with these two landscapes [England and Guyana]. Add to that a U.S. experience and a black perspective. For me, imaginative writing is about historical recovery and finding forms to shape memory. Discovery is a part of the equation, too. The oxygen for all this is love and loss. (*Contemporary Authors*, vol. 148, p.102)

Fred D'Aguiar was a guest of the Adelaide Writers Festival in 1996. He lives at various times in the United Kingdom, the United States and the Caribbean. He has held a variety of university teaching positions including visiting fellow at Cambridge University, England 1989-1990, visiting writer at Amherst College, MA 1992-1994, and assistant professor of English at Bates College, Lewiston, ME 1994-1995. He is currently professor of English at the University of Miami.

NOTES ON

GENRE, STYLE AND STRUCTURE

The Longest Memory is a highly unusual text, both generically and technically. One way of looking at it is to say that it is an historical novel, a story set in another time and place (the slave era, on a plantation in the southern American state of Virginia). The author, we know, has researched the period and location, and created his fictional narrative out of the 'real' events of his chosen context. Yet it quickly becomes obvious that what interests him is not really the historical detail, the period 'colour' or exotic aspects of his subject. He is far more absorbed in the 'political' issues revealed in the story – specifically the problem of who had power and who had not, and how this distorted everything about life in that situation. It goes further than this. As we read, we understand that the political issues share centre stage with psychological, moral and even philosophical problems, of real complexity. D'Aguiar is more concerned with the conflicting perceptions, beliefs about what is right and wrong, and different versions of the 'reality' of the events, than he is the superficial facts of slavery. A summary of this novel does it no justice. It is not just about the whipping to death of a young slave man and the traumatic reaction of his adopted father. It is about the whole system, the type of racist thinking involved, and the confusion and complications on all sides, that arise in such unnatural circumstances. It is about the nature of remembering, and how people interpret their world. The text is an historical novel, but it is also political, psychological, moral and philosophical in its concerns. It would be a mistake to define it too narrowly.

Technically, we must start with the author's choice of narrative mode. Other modern writers have chosen to tell their story in the voices of different characters. Two famous examples are *The Sound and the Fury* (1929), by the famous American author William Faulkner, in which four voices go over the same events from their individual perspectives, and *The Collector* (1963), by Englishman John Fowles, in which the two protagonists, the psychopath and his victim, relate the story from their own points of view. Choosing to tell a story from different narrative viewpoints is a real challenge for a writer. He must somehow sustain the reader's interest, despite the fact that the narrators are in a sense telling the same story. The technique also tests the reader, who must keep track of who is who, and how their different viewpoints all match together. *The Longest Memory* is extraodinary in that it uses not two, or even four, but ten different voices. Why? To show that the 'truth' is not any one person's. It is far too easy, the author has said, to adopt stereotypical views of something as notorious as slavery, whereas what he wanted was to provoke 'a more sophisticated response'. While the voices of the various first-person narrators sound authentic, it is important to remember that they were in fact created by D'Aguiar and that the text was written in the 1990s, not in the late eighteenth/early nineteenth century. Therefore, while the views of the characters are appropriate to the period in which the novel is set, the message of the author is from a late twentieth century perspective. It is most important – and this needs particular underlining – not to confuse the views of any particular narrator with those of the author.

The structure of *The Longest Memory* needs comment too. D'Aguiar does not tell the central story in a linear, chronological fashion. Instead, the novel begins with a prologue called 'Remembering', set in the 'present' of Whitechapel's extreme old age, shortly before his death, and it ends with an epilogue called 'Forgetting', which ends at his death. In between are twelve 'chapters' (or narrative fragments), almost all of them 'flashbacks', to periods as early as the previous generation ('Sanders Senior') and one a leap forward in time ('Great Granddaughter') to the moment immediately after Whitechapel's death. Not only do the different fragments come from different voices (several reappearing more than once), but they differ in style. The forms in which the narratives are embedded include narrative prose, diary entries, poetry and newspaper editorials. Some are poetic in style, some blunt and prosaic, as suits the character concerned. This characteristically 'postmodern' structure, using different types of writing to express divergent viewpoints, makes the novel more interesting to read, as well as allowing the author to use appropriate language forms for each character. One of the important effects of this style is that each character has a personal voice and is portrayed as a complex human being, responding to circumstances as his/her nature and upbringing dictate. *The Longest Memory* thus avoids being a simple novel of 'goodies' and 'baddies'. The slaves, the plantation owner, the overseer and the minor characters are shown as complex individuals, not simple stereotypes. It also conveys a view of reality as being personal, fluid and relative rather than a fixed entity. For instance, we are invited to see that there is no 'correct' view of the fatal whipping of Chapel, but a variety of different viewpoints, all valid for the people who express them. Shifting between different narrators allows the author to express individual points of view, rather than an omniscient (all-knowing) narrator who tells the whole story.

Why does D'Aguiar not tell the story in traditional chronological order (the order of clock time)? Why begin with the old man some time after the whipping incident, move back to the whipping incident, then unfold the events leading to the tragedy, moving backwards and forwards in time, covering the same events and the same periods from different points of view? Because, the author has said, that this approach replicates more exactly what history (whether public or personal) is really like.

> I think that viewing history with a single voice, going back in time and
> carving out this straight road to the present, is a bit of an illusion because
> history is full of upheavals. It doesn't necessarily progress. There are
> backward steps, depending on what happens to the country or the region. I
> think apart from upheavals and backward leaps, there is the sense that
> history is full of contradictions, and those contradictions are best shown
> by voices contradicting each other. (Interview with the author, cited
> above)

Just as, in a person's mind, time is malleable, with instant imaginative jumps back into memory, and forward into speculation, so in this novel the 'simultaneous universes' of the different characters' realities are presented for our contemplation. Because the main story is 'rehearsed' or dealt with several times, though from different perspectives, it is not difficult to follow the sequence of events.

The actual time setting of the novel begins with Sanders' first diary entry on 12 January 1796 and ends with the old slave's death some time after the last editorial in *The Virginian* on 23 June 1810. This was a period in which attitudes towards slavery were changing, and which saw the beginning of the movement in North America to abolish slavery. The views expressed by plantation owners in the novel are therefore part of a determined effort to resist any basis, theoretical or practical, for the abolition of slavery, which they saw as essential to the continued existence of the big plantations and of their affluent lifestyle.

Finally, let us note that the simple language of the characters and the brevity of the novel do not imply simple ideas. The issues and ideas are complex and unforgettable. As we acknowledged earlier, this is a text with multiple layers. *The Longest Memory*, like most black literature, may be a political novel, with the impossibility of retaining humanity within an inhuman system as its main argument. However, it is also an exploration of the universal theme of human responses to oppression, of the psychological motivations underlying personal choices, of the moral and philsophical dilemmas with which people often have to cope.

BACKGROUND NOTES

SLAVERY IN AMERICA

Slavery has existed throughout history. At least as early as the beginning of settled agricultural communities, slaves, usually prisoners of war, were used by many communities. Both the ancient Greeks and Romans had slaves. In the Roman Empire, they were an integral part of the social order.

The conquest of Central and South America by Europeans in the 1400s, and the subsequent development of sugar and coffee plantations in the 'New World', created a huge demand for field workers. Free labour was either not available or was too expensive, so slaves were brought in from Africa. The Portugese were the first to use captured labour, starting in 1444. They were soon imitated by the Spanish, and by the early 1600s the British had moved into the slave trade in a major way. The system was brutal. White men with guns, aided by local collaborators, raided villages in Africa. These were military-style operations, in which vast numbers of individuals – men, women and children – were caught at gunpoint, chained, taken to the coast and transported by ship to the new plantation states. Many died in the inhuman conditions of the sea voyage, from suffocation, disease or other traumas. On arrival, the survivors were either traded for goods or auctioned to the highest bidder, like cattle.

In North America, the first African slaves arrived in Jamestown, Virginia in 1619. Laws to legalise the trade followed, and over time the owners' complete rights of possession over their black workers were institutionalised. The trade increased rapidly. It is estimated, for example, that more than 70,000 slaves were brought from Africa in the year 1790. By 1800, there were nearly a million slaves in North America (96% in the south). A census taken in 1860 showed that there were 3,953,760 slaves. Most lived in the southern states, where they were used to work cotton and tobacco plantations. The northern states were largely based around manufacturing industry, so the economy of these states was not reliant on slavery.

However, while in the minds of southern American plantation owners slavery was both essential and morally defensible, elsewhere the practice was as more and more repugnant. The slave trade was outlawed in the British Empire in 1807, and in the northern states of America was gradually abolished over the period 1787-1804 (almost the same period as *The Longest Memory*, 1796-1810). After the War of Independence (1775-1783), which resulted in the United States cutting ties with Britain and becoming a republic, America had rapidly developed its democratic ideology. The Declaration of Independence in particular, with its commitment to the principles of liberty, brotherhood and the right to personal fulfilment, was perceived as being quite contrary to the precepts of slavery. By 1842, the British, Americans and others had signed the Ashburton Treaty, which went so far as to station ships off the coast of Africa to physically prevent the slave trade. Public opinion had finally solidified into fierce opposition to the inhumanity of the system.

However, the southern states refused to give up slavery. They dismissed 'abolitionists' as 'Yankee' (northern) radicals, and clung to the system for another forty years after abolition in the north, in the face of mounting criticism. The end came finally in the early 1860s. Both newly elected Republican President Abraham Lincoln and the US congress were taking an increasingly hard line attitude on slavery. Lincoln had been born in a slave state (Kentucky), but had always despised the practice. Feeling that their cause was becoming hopeless in a congress dominated by the north and under a President opposed to slavery, a Confederacy (political alliance) of southern states broke away from the rest of the Union, and set up Richmond, Virginia as its rebel capital. There was a stalemate for two months. Then Confederate guns fired on a Union ship supplying a government fort in South Carolina. At that point, Lincoln ordered the troops in.

America was plunged into a bloodbath, the Civil War (1861-1865). At first the south made headway, and the speedy victory expected by Lincoln and his advisors never materialised. Indeed, because of its military skill and because it was fighting on home ground, the Confederate army had significant victories. But gradually, the superior strength of the Union prevailed. There were 27,000,000 people in the Union states, as against just 9,000,000 (of whom nearly half were slaves) in the Confederacy. The north had a strong industrial base and the manpower to sustain a large army. Finally, the decimated Confederate army was forced to surrender. On 9 April 1865, after nearly four years of butchery, General Robert E Lee handed over his sword, and the conflict was at an end. It had been a disastrous war. Over 620,000 men were dead and as many again wounded (out of a total population of 35,000,000!). One in four Confederate soldiers had perished. It was a trauma which deeply scared the south, and from which the new United States took a long time to recover.

However, the Civil War had one positive outcome. In 1863, Abraham Lincoln's famous Emancipation Proclamation had declared American blacks 'then, henceforth and forever free'. In January 1865, his antislavery amendment to the Constitution was passed. By one of those tragic ironies of history, this great man never lived to see the results of his enlightened actions. Five days after the end of the war, he was shot in the head by a southern extremist, John Wilkes Booth. He died the following day. However, despite Lincoln's assassination, his actions, and the defeat of the Confederate south, marked the official end of slavery in America.

BACKGROUND NOTES

BLACK WRITING

During the twentieth century, 'black consciousness' has grown rapidly, and the rise of activist movements (committed to political change) has been reflected in black literature, both in the United States and in Australia. In both countries, we can recognise the common themes of oppression, loss of family, fear of violence committed by whites, poor living conditions and harsh punishments for black people under the justice system.

Early writing about the plight of black people in both countries was by white authors. Classic novels about slavery include Harriet Beecher Stowe's *Uncle Tom's Cabin*, published in 1852, and *To Kill a Mockingbird* by Harper Lee, published in 1960.

In Australia, Aboriginal literature began as a 'cry for justice' directed at white society, based on the fight for equality. However, black Australian writing has now moved towards the search for roots and 'a literature of understanding less committed to explaining Aboriginal individuals to a predominantly white readership' (Mudrooroo, *Writing from the Fringe*, 1990). Novels such as Mudrooroo's *Wild Cat Falling*, Sally Morgan's *My Place*, and the poetry of Oodgeroo Noonuccal (Kath Walker) and Jack Davis are significant landmarks in this movement.

American black writing has followed a similar pattern, moving from 'cry for justice' literature to the exploration of human experience and behaviour during a terrible period in history. Novelists like Toni Morrison, the first black writer to win the Nobel Prize for Literature (1993) have created novels which explore the experience of African Americans in depth and with real subtlety.

The Longest Memory is part of this new literature of understanding. The novel is an exploration of the way people respond when placed in the context of slavery. Both masters and slaves have choices to make about the kinds of people they are and how they fulfil the roles in which they find themselves. *The Longest Memory* is more than a political novel about the evils of slavery. It is an exploration of human motivation and the way people make choices which influence not only their actions but their self-image. It is a modern novel about how people create themselves and reconcile their views of the world with their personal reality.

SUMMARY

COMMENTARY

PROLOGUE: REMEMBERING

The narrator (Whitechapel the slave) reflects on memory and the pain caused by remembering. He tells us about the pointless death by whipping of a boy, one whom he loved as a son.

We learn that since the day of the whipping he has decided to have no name. He also tells us, in a poignant demonstration of pain, that since the boy's death he doesn't cry any more.

The prologue plunges us into the tormented consciousness of the central character, Whitechapel the slave. From the start we know what the novel is to be about – slavery. The word 'slave' is used on the first page, and the whipping of the boy has obviously had a profound effect on the old man. For Whitechapel, something appalling has happened, which has trans-formed him. He has moved from a state of love and relative contentment to one of unbearable grief. He has been drained of emotions. There are bodily symptoms of trauma (aching, bleeding). Most striking of all, he has decided to reject his own identity.

At this point we don't know what has happened or why Whitechapel is so deeply affected, though the whipping is plainly at the heart of it. We know that there is a story to be told, and this opening passage engages our interest immediately, making us wonder why the boy's death had such a dramatic effect on the old man. It also, with hindsight, raises key issues – the burden of memory, the tragedy of slavery, the problem of how a person reacts to injustice, the problem of judgement, and so on. It is worth coming back to this short prologue after finishing the novel, to see again how the author's major preoccupations are present from the outset.

CHAPTER ONE: WHITECHAPEL

The narrator, Whitechapel the slave, describes the vicious 200 stroke whipping of the boy that he was forced to watch, and the effect it had on him. He began by feeling the boy's pain, but eventually 'learned how to live without being hurt by life'. He learned, in short, to block out his feelings. The boy was still alive when he was cut down, but the narrator had seen something in the boy's eyes half way through the punishment which showed him that the spirit within had died. The boy had surren-dered life and crossed into the next world.

We learn that the narrator has buried two wives and most of his children, though he is surrounded by grandchildren and great-grandchil-dren. Unable to laugh, he has earned the nickname 'Sour-face'. His grand-children see him as a laughing stock and a burden.

He describes the death of his second wife from fever, followed by the death of his son the next day from the whipping. The son ran away after the death of his mother (Whitechapel's wife). Whitechapel, who believed the boy would inevitably be caught and killed on the spot, told the master, Mr Whitechapel, where his son was to be found and begged for leniency. The master left the plantation, leaving orders with the over-seer's deputy that the boy was to be locked up until his return. However, at dusk, the deputy left the plantation and was absent when the boy was brought back in chains.

The overseer, Sanders, who had been in charge of the tracking, ordered the 200 lashes to be carried out immediately, despite Whitechapel's pleas. The other slaves blamed Whitechapel for giving up his son, and the son also blamed his father. Whitechapel objected, was hit by the overseer and threatened with a whipping alongside his son. He offered to take his son's place, but the overseer merely ordered that he be held down and forced to watch.

We are aware that this event took place some time in the past. Since then, he lives on grieving, into old age.

What is perhaps most poignant is the old slave believing he will receive fair treatment if he is obedient and respectful. He is senior slave on the plantation, and has obeyed the system for years. Yet we see that he is not given any special consideration at all. We learn through Whitechapel's reflections that he believes there are two kinds of possible responses to slavery: the respectful obedience he himself shows, and the rebellion of young slaves like his 'son'. We realise, as Whitechapel does not, that his responses are those of one who has been a slave so long that he accepts his master's view of himself as inferior, as one who must obey, respect and accept ill-treatment in order to save himself from abuse or death. He identifies with his master's interests, and sees the avoidance of trouble as being his primary duty.

Whitechapel has deluded himself into believing that if he behaves with dignity and reason, he will be treated with respect. The events of that night showed him otherwise, destroying his belief in himself and his image of himself as the faithful and respected servant. We understand now why he repudiates his name, which is identical to the master's. He rejects, belatedly, the system which killed the boy, and of which he was such a compliant part. Being a model slave, being 'Whitechapel' (the name is symbolic of his being the master's obliging servant) was unintentionally the reason for the death of his son. The silent accusations of the other slaves, together with his son's blame, turn out to be justified. The old slave's view of the world, developed over years, has been shattered by the whipping of the boy he thought of as a son.

CHAPTER TWO: MR WHITECHAPEL

This chapter reveals the viewpoint of Mr Whitechapel, owner of the plantation, on his return after the whipping.

His first remarks are addressed to Whitechapel the slave. He tells Whitechapel that the boy brought about his own death through rebellion, and argues that the punishment was just. He orders Whitechapel to apologise for questioning the overseer and says that they agreed it was Whitechapel's responsibility to save the boy from himself. His (Whitechapel's) failure alone was responsible for the boy's death.

After the old slave leaves, Mr Whitechapel turns to Sanders, the overseer. The slaves are now disgruntled and rebellion is likely as a result of the boy's death. Mr Whitechapel reprimands Sanders for disobeying his orders, and fines him an amount equal to the boy's monetary value (as a slave in his prime). He also criticises the brutality of Sanders' treatment of Whitechapel, in having his son 'whipped to death before his eyes'. Mr Whitechapel argues against cruelty and rough handling of slaves on humanitarian but also practical grounds.

He goes on to speak of the hard work done to retain Whitechapel's obedience on a previous occasion. He reveals that Sanders' father raped Whitechapel's second wife, and that the boy was actually Sanders' half-brother. This was kept secret and Whitechapel raised the boy as his own, but Sanders Senior was supposed to have told his son. Whitechapel, Mr Whitechapel and the boy's mother believed he had done so. However, the revelation is clearly a surprise to Sanders Junior.

Mr Whitechapel ends with a prayer, shared with Sanders, for God's guidance in dealing with slaves.

Mr Whitechapel, like everyone else, shifts the blame for the boy's death onto Whitechapel the slave. In his eyes, Whitechapel had agreed to try to prevent the boy from running away, and had failed. It is an extraordinary moral shift, and typical somehow of a regime entirely constructed for the benefit of one side. Even the blame is a burden to be loaded onto the powerless black man. Mr Whitechapel is not capable of seeing that the system itself, which he personifies, is the real villain. That is what caused the boy to be whipped to death – not the hapless slave who only thought he was doing the best thing for the boy. Although we will later see Mr Whitechapel as far from being a monster, this first confrontation with the callousness of his position is a shock, and a significant one.

Note that Mr Whitechapel thinks of the boy in monetary terms. It is not a personal thing, but business. For him the death can be remedied by fining Sanders, a jarring note in comparison to Whitechapel's grief. It reminds us that slaves were like livestock, valued per head according to age and physical condition. Mr Whitechapel also comments to Sanders, that the slaves are 'inferiors', having 'lesser faculties' and therefore suited to slavery. It is vital to understand that we are not supposed to accept his beliefs, but to see them as racist statements without foundation in fact, typical of the beliefs of the time which allowed slavery to be condoned.

The revelation that the boy was Sanders' half-brother is another tragic twist. A white man, because he is capable of accepting a system which allows such savagery, has inadvertently killed his own brother, who had the misfortune (in this time) to be born black. What the novel is arguing, subtextually, is that in a symbolic or metaphoric way, white men and black men are brothers, and should not harm one another. Here we see the system violating that ancient moral law in the tragic death of one literal brother at the hands of another. It is the system which is guilty, though Sanders was the precise instrument of this cruelty. We understand now why Whitechapel regarded the boy as being 'like a son'. We also understand the way the system binds both oppressors and oppressed in pain and guilt. Mr Whitechapel, dimly grasping how their lives are woven together, senses the wretchedness of which they are all a part.

After such scandalous revelations, the prayer at the end seems (to us) like blatant hypocrisy, yet from Mr Whitechapel's point of view he treating his slaves in a reasonable and morally defensible way. That it was the conventional morality of that time, one in which. We realise with a shock that God was seen to condone slavery.

CHAPTER THREE: SANDERS SENIOR

This chapter is in the form of a diary kept by Sanders Senior, overseer for Mr Whitechapel Senior, father of the current owner. The diary entries, which begin on 12 January 1796 and end on 30 November 1797, take us back to the conception and birth of the boy who is later to be whipped to death.

We learn that Sanders' wife Caroline died giving birth to his son, Sanders Junior. The son cried when Sanders told him his mother died in childbirth. Sanders Senior does not want his son to become an overseer. He dreams of his son becoming a scientist or philosopher, or even a poet.

Sanders buys a new girl at the slave market. She says she is fifteen but he thinks she is about twenty-two. He soon makes her his cook. In August, Whitechapel obtains permission from Mr Whitechapel to marry the cook. Sanders, however, has also taken a fancy to the new girl, and delays the marriage, saying he must first find another cook. On Christmas Eve, Sanders rapes her. She asks to be allowed to marry Whitechapel immediately, in return for not telling anyone. On January 1st, the marriage takes place. On January 9, unable to control his lust, Sanders rapes her again. This time she tells Mr Whitechapel. Whitechapel is persuaded to say nothing and to keep her as his wife. She is taken away from Sanders' house to cook in Mr Whitechapel's house.

In May, a runaway is caught and whipped (200 lashes) by Sanders and his deputy. The runaway subsequently dies. Whitechapel says the death is from the whipping, but Sanders argues that it was a fever, not the whipping, which caused the death. Mr Whitechapel's two sons are present for the whipping.

In September, Whitechapel's wife gives birth to a son who is black but otherwise looks like Sanders. Mr Whitechapel forces Sanders to marry a woman he dislikes in order to avoid further scandalous rumours.

There are many comments in Sanders' diary which reveal his attitude towards the slaves. It is notable that they are similar views to those expressed by his son in the previous chapter. Sanders believes that Mr Whitechapel is too lenient and that beating is the way to teach the slaves their place. He follows Mr Whitechapel's orders to use the whip or stick but not boots or fists on the slaves, though he doesn't agree with the policy. He also believes that slaves should not be fed so much, disagreeing with Mr Whitechapel, who says they look too thin and orders more rations.

His white supremacist attitude is chilling in its matter-of-factness. Nowhere is this so clear as in his cold-blooded use of the cook for his sexual needs, not once, but twice, before he is forced, by outside pressure to stop. The terrible admission, 'I did not enjoy myself so much as relieve myself', is a reminder of how absolutely callous he is. Of all the characters in The Longest Memory*, this man, and his actions, and the consequences of his actions, perhaps best sum up the diabolic system which made him and them possible.*

The story of the runaway helps us to understand why Whitechapel was so fearful when his son ran away (years later), and why he wanted to save him from a punishment such as he had already witnessed, and its fatal aftermath. Note that on this occasion the other slaves are angry with the runaway because he brings them punishments. In the later case, significantly, the other slaves are sympathetic to Chapel's attempt to escape. This suggests a change in attitudes over the years, one with which Whitechapel has not caught up.

We see here a little of Sanders Junior as a child, revealing a softer side. He cried about his mother's death, and followed the kindly Whitechapel around. However, we also see the role model who is to be the strongest influence on the boy's life: his father, who is brutal with the slaves, ignorant, and despicably self-indulgent at the expense of others.

There is irony in Sanders Senior's determination that his son will not become an overseer, but something much better. We already know that his son does become an overseer, much like his father. There is also irony in Sanders' dream, because it is not to be his legitimate, white son, but his black son, Chapel, who will become the philosopher and poet.

CHAPTER FOUR: COOK

This short chapter is narrated by the cook who became Whitechapel's second wife. After the rape, she wanted to kill herself, but Whitechapel rescued her and enabled her to continue to live on the plantation without shame. Whitechapel not only saved her life and her child's, but was even responsible for having the overseer fined and made to apologise, as well as for Mr Whitechapel's kindness towards her.

She admires Whitechapel, is grateful for his protection, and vows to bear him many sons and see him die contented. She envisages herself in old age surrounded by their sons after Whitechapel dies (he is much older than she is).

We cannot help noticing the contrast between the kind of man Whitechapel is (protective, considerate, trustworthy, gentle), and the kind of man we have just seen in the overseer Sanders Senior (selfish, weak, self-indulgent, brutal, careless towards others). The chapter makes a strong comment about slavery and the injustice of a system which gives an inferior man authority over a superior one, just because he is white.

It is important to understand that once the cook was raped and became pregnant to the overseer, despite her complete innocence, she would have been an object of shame and scandal. Without Whitechapel, she may have been sent away, sold, or even killed, to cover up the problem of her unmarried pregnancy. No-one wanted an illegitimate and unwanted child. In a no doubt deliberate reference to yet another form of oppression – that of women – D'Aguiar reminds us that in those days men had complete authority over women, who had strict moral restrictions placed upon their conduct that did not really apply to men, in a sexist system partly paralleling that by which white people had authority over black.

There is an element of tragic irony in her grateful predictions of a happy old age. We already know that she does not bear Whitechapel sons, and that he outlives her, to die in misery after the death of the child who was not even his own. Instead of the contented old age she imagines, she

*will die in fact young of fever, because of being refused medical attention,
and Whitechapel will live on alone, derided and shamed, outliving most
of his daughters. There is a poignant sadness in the reality that instead of
the happiness she wanted to bring Whitechapel, she unwittingly brought
tragedy, sacrifice and shame.*

CHAPTER FIVE: CHAPEL

This chapter is written in verse (rhyming couplets). It is the voice of Chapel
(the name shortened by his mother, to avoid confusion with his father),
discussing his life, his mother, Whitechapel, his relationship with Lydia
and his dreams of freedom.

He explains how Whitechapel used reason, not beating, to teach
him the right ways to behave. He writes of happy days spent in the master's kitchen with his mother, while she cooked and fed him delicacies.
He writes about the master's youngest daughter, Lydia, who taught him to
read and write, sworn to secrecy because it was forbidden. He records the
day Mr Whitechapel caught them and beat him with his belt for learning
to read.

Forbidden to see each other, he and Lydia meet secretly at night,
turning their backs so that they were technically not disobeying the de-
cree never to see one another again. She memorised passages of literature
for him, while he composed poetry to say aloud for her.

Chapel also records a conversation with Whitechapel, who talks to
him about there being two kinds of slaves, obedient and rebellious. His
adopted father feared for him because he refused to submit, although he
brushed off the old man's advice.

Lydia persuades him to try to escape, and finally, after his mother
dies, he runs away. The chapter ends with his joy in being free.

*The relationship between Lydia and Chapel has a Romeo and Juliet qual-
ity, of innocent love forbidden by families due to society's constraints. As
with Romeo and Juliet, we see the genuine commitment of two 'soulmates',
whose intellectual and spiritual compatibility argue very strongly against
the man-made barriers of race and caste. Why should they not love one
another? They have not been corrupted or twisted by prejudice. Only the
system keeps them apart, the same evil system that results in every other
tragedy in this story. But in consequence of the system, as with Romeo
and Juliet, their love was doomed to fail. What they wished for, a life of
freedom and equality, was, for the time and place, a complete impossibility.*

SUMMARY AND COMMENTARY

Just as with Romeo and Juliet, where the malice of the feuding families turned their love to tragedy, so here too, the corruption and restriction of the system turned Chapel and Lydia's love, innocence and hope for the future, into death and despair.

Forbidden to be with the girl he loves, and losing his adored mother, Chapel, rashly but understandably, runs away. In this escape, he feels 'joy, not fear'. However, we already know the outcome of this escape. What he thought was a solution becomes the prelude to a tragic end. Paradoxically, we share the father's fear, while also understanding the son's joy. We empathise with Chapel, wanting him to be happy, but we know, with Whitechapel, that his freedom will not last. It is the fearless joy of a young man, confident in his ability to make the world fit his dreams, contrasting the fear of the older, wiser man who has seen it all before.

The fact that this chapter is written in rhyming couplets is, naturally, significant. The tragedy of Whitechapel, an intelligent, kindly man caught in an inhumane system, is sharpened in the vision we now have of Chapel, his adopted son. What do the reading and writing tell us about Chapel? Here was a child with absolutely no literacy in his own background, who 'picked up' reading as if it were a game. He was capable, not just of writing, but of writing poetry. He was, we must conclude, a gifted child of prodigious intelligence. How terrible, we are invited to see, that such abilities should be forced to bury themselves. The slave system, the racist mentality, tried to crush everything in those it deemed inferior: feeling and learning, as well as physical and political freedom. It was slavery of the mind as well as slavery of the body.

As the character of Chapel is revealed, we become increasingly aware of the significance of the name 'Whitechapel', shared by three of the main characters. It is an ironic name, suggestive of the 'whited sepulchre', white on the outside but rotten within. The name conjures up a pastoral image of a white chapel surrounded by green fields. There is an irony in calling an African slave by a name so resonant of English-American pastorals. The shortening to Chapel suggests holiness, purity, worship, love, and perhaps we are intended to attribute these qualities to the young innocent Chapel, who became a sacrifice to racial oppression. Remembering that Fred D'Aguiar is an acclaimed poet whose use of language has been praised by some of the best critics, it is reasonable to suggest that the use of the name is intentionally subtle wordplay.

CHAPTER SIX: PLANTATION OWNERS

This chapter gives us the thoughts of Mr Whitechapel, whom it depicts visiting the plantation owners Club after the whipping, although he expects (and receives) scorn and derision, and the voices of the other white bosses at the Club.

Mr Whitechapel insists that he is not one of the oppressors, despite the whipping. The other plantation owners see the whipping and death of the slave as a good thing, a warning to others. They mock Mr Whitechapel, quoting his own words about slavery, now seen as hollow in the light of the whipping, and call him a fool and a hypocrite. It is not the whipping they disapprove of, it is Mr Whitechapel's idea that slaves are human and should be shown respect. Mr Whitechapel defends his beliefs as based on Christianity. The others say he is an abolitionist (one who wants to see slavery abolished).

Mr Whitechapel, in response, maintains that the slave who bears his name is 'living proof that slaves are our equal in every way'. Eventually, after hedging around the matter for a time, he tells the other owners of the rape and the relationship between Sanders and the boy he killed. (They were half brothers with the same father.) He tells of Whitechapel's nobility and obedience in accepting the woman as his wife and in not revealing the secret even when the boy was whipped to death. The other owners want to buy Whitechapel, and Mr Whitechapel's way of running his plantation is vindicated. He leaves the Club feeling the respect of the other owners and with his good name restored.

In this chapter, we are invited to see Mr Whitechapel in a different light. We understand the enormous peer group pressure to which he is subjected. Being the only kindly slave owner in his district has made him the subject of contempt and harassment. Even a man of good will had a well nigh impossible task sticking to his principles in that time and place. This tension is visible in the contradictory stance he takes on the whipping. He seems to be wanting to say both that one should treat slaves with kindness and humanity, but also that the whipping was a necessary deterrent, though he doesn't like the practice. Is this hypocrisy, or just perplexity, the clash between a fundamentally good man and an evil system?

The other slave owners argue that Mr. Whitechapel's soft treatment of his slaves encouraged the escape attempt, and not really a kindness, because it encourages them to believe they are equals and to try to escape or rebel, which is then punished severely. By accusing Mr Whitechapel of being an abolitionist, they are suggesting that his way of treating his slaves and his argument that they are equal to whites will eventually lead to the end of slavery. Their own self-interest in this (maintaining their wealth and status) is a key motive, which we should note, though they dress it up as a principle.

Mr Whitechapel wants to belong, to be accepted, despite his different views on the treatment of slaves. He is, after all, still a slave-owner, a member of the Club, one of them. In the end, his way of treating his slaves is vindicated by the loyalty of Whitechapel – 'beyond the requisition of duty' – which is seen as a remarkable accomplishment achieved. Clearly, treating slaves with brutality may ensure obedience, but it will be sullen obedience, not willing co-operation. It could be argued, then, that Mr Whitechapel's way of managing slaves is more subtle, but in the end more complete and successful, than the brutality of the other slave owners.

CHAPTER SEVEN: LYDIA

This chapter is narrated by Lydia (Mr Whitechapel's only daughter). She recalls when she first began teaching Chapel to read and write. We see Chapel through Lydia's eyes as a boy who has a natural curiosity and enjoys learning.

Chapel is a quick learner, and once he is able to read, Lydia teaches him to write their shared surname: Whitechapel. Lydia asks the cook why she shortens the boy's name to Chapel. The cook says because it is confusing to have both father and son with the same name.

It is forbidden for a slave to learn to read and write, yet the boy is curious and intelligent. There is a simple innocence about this relationship between a bright boy and a broad-minded girl which is enormously appealing. It reminds us (if we think about what is happening) how brutally unnatural was the socially-imposed difference of owner and slave, and the assumption that slaves should not learn to read and write. However, while Lydia and Chapel, two innocent children, can ignore social restraints, clearly sooner or later, the artificial adult world will intervene. We feel the weight in the irony (knowledge which we already have) of how the reading project will end – in tragedy. Although they share the same name, the gap between Chapel and Lydia is a fatal one.

We should note that the issue of the rights of slaves, and specifically whether a slave should be allowed to learn to read and write, is here raised by a dissenting white person. We must remind ourselves that not all Americans at this time, or even all southerners, believed in the slave system. At this point, Lydia's opposition to the regime is not clearly articulated (as it will be in later chapters), but her implicit belief in the right of all to literacy and knowledge it represents, though she is part of a system which outlaws it for black people, is to be noted as a most important sign of an alternative point of view, and morality.

CHAPTER EIGHT: COOK

From the previous chapter narrated by Cook, we know her as the raped woman who became Whitechapel's wife. Now she is the mother of Chapel.

She thinks about the two cooking pots she tends, her master's and her own. The master's has the best food, but her own is for the people she loves: her husband and her son.

She hears Chapel reading to Lydia, the 'darling of the house'. His voice sounds like the master's. She is afraid, terrified by the forbidden learning, yet also intensely proud of her son. She worries, and considers telling her husband, but she knows he will stop the reading because he, too, believes it is not a slave's place to read. She thinks her son deserves to be allowed this pleasure. Worry and fear vie with pride and happiness and not wanting to take away something precious to him. She decides not to tell.

In cook's perspective, we see another dissenter. The issue here is quality of life versus mere survival. Whitechapel, her husband, has made an art of survival through obedience to the system, and in return is treated with a degree of respect. But her son has the potential for more than survival, and she wants to see him fulfil a bigger dream. We know where this will eventually lead, but we understand the mother's wish to see her brilliant son do more than just live on as the illiterate possession of a white man. It is another example of the way natural justice is contrary to the code of slavery, and again illustrates the cruelty of what was allowed and what was not.

CHAPTER NINE: LYDIA

One day, while listening to Chapel read, Lydia realises she loves Chapel. It is the day Mr Whitechapel finds them reading together. He beats Chapel with his belt, then forbids him to come into the house. He tells Lydia she was wrong to teach Chapel reading and writing which he can never use.

Lydia argues with her father about the injustice of the law against slaves reading and writing. Perhaps next century, he says, it might be possible, but that leaves her with no hope for the future.

Because she loves Chapel, Lydia and is miserable at the loss of their time together. However, Chapel's mother tells Lydia about a special place to sit where she can watch the heavens. She goes, and Chapel meets her there. He has promised not to read or write, and refuses her offer of books and paper, because that would break the rules set by her father. They sit back to back, so that they cannot see each other. He asks her to memorise something from a book, while he will compose poetry for her. That way they are technically not disobeying. They continue to meet on clear nights, but they both know there is no future in their relationship on the plantation.

Once again, the evil of the system is underpinned by our powerful feelings for the characters. Here, it is primarily Lydia with whom we identify, and her painful realisation that her love for Chapel cannot be realised. She is a plantation owner's daughter. He is a slave. Their love must be kept secret. The evils of slavery are at their most obvious here, where a naturally developing love between two young people is made doomed by the fact that one of them is a slave. Marriage is impossible. Even friendship must be shared in secret and cannot last. It is clear that the inequality between slave and master, black and white, is artificially created by society. The young, who have not yet had this engraved in their minds, or their thoughts poisoned with prejudice, find it easy and natural to relate to each other as equals. Despite their hopes though, like so many others, they will be the victims of exactly that prejudice.

CHAPTER TEN: LYDIA

Lydia grows into a young woman. Possible suitors visit. She compares them with Chapel and finds them coarse, boasting, lacking his wit, charm and sensitivity. She refuses them and wishes Chapel was white.

Chapel has now memorised a body of literature including Milton, Spenser, Shakespeare, Homer.

Lydia's brother Thomas returns from the north with stories of white women living with black men. He is disgusted, but Lydia is hopeful for herself and Chapel. She persuades Chapel to run away to the north. He is reluctant to disobey his father and hers, and to leave his mother, but his love for Lydia is stronger and he agrees to do it after his mother dies.

Lydia asks her brother to take her on his next trip north. She explains the plan to her father, disguising it as wanting to look further afield for a suitor. Her mother refuses to allow it, until Lydia suggests she should come too.

Lydia and Chapel dream of freedom, of living together, and having children, while Chapel will make a living writing verse.

The relationship between Lydia and Chapel is characterised by idealism, by an almost childish hope that life will be as it ought to be, not as it is. For slaves, such dreams were rarely fulfilled, and only at great cost to themselves and others. Lydia, in her naivety, has fed Chapel dreams which may be admirable, but which are also dangerous, and has persuaded him to risk his life. Note that there is no risk to her at any time. Just as she was unable to save him from being belted by her father, so she will be unable to save him from the consequences if he is caught trying to escape. We sympathise with their dreams, but we already know for the outcome for Chapel, and wonder about the tragic mixed blessing of Lydia's love.

We recognise, as Lydia and Chapel do not, the ghetto-style lives of poverty which arose from mixed marriages. We also realise that even if she had managed to escape from her mother and marry Chapel, her brothers would undoubtedly have come and taken her back, and killed Chapel. Escaped slaves still belonged to their owners. They could be caught in the north and taken back to the south, or destroyed (as an animal might be by its owner). All this knowledge we bring, in sadness, to Lydia's innocent fantasies.

CHAPTER ELEVEN: THE VIRGINIAN

This chapter is a series of editorials from *The Virginian*, during the period between December 1809 and June 1810. [Although fictional, they express views typical of the time.]

The editorials cover a variety of issues relating to slavery, set in a time when the practice was being questioned by those in the northern states, and at the same time was vigorously defended by slave owners in the south. The defence of slavery as a Christian and proper practice depended on the idea that slaves were sub-human (akin to animals) and therefore not to be treated like other people. This assumption underlies many of the comments made in the editorials. Indeed, one of the early editorials states: 'The premise of buying and selling Africans is built upon precepts concerning their difference from our good selves'.

The editorials cover such matters as beating slaves, selling mothers and children separately, the punishment of runaways (200 lashes is recommended), the fate of old slaves, temptations posed to male owners and overseers by young female slaves, Christianity and slavery, firmness versus kindness in running a plantation, whether slavery will ever end, the idea of paying slaves, literacy and slavery, white women in relationships with black men.

Firstly, let us note that all of the discussion is from the viewpoint of the plantation owners and white society. None concerns what is best for the slaves. The editorials are conservative and inclined to express opinions suited to the majority of readers and social mores of the time. Only rarely are the views expressed truly controversial, though the subjects often are. The editorials reflect the views of the plantation owners, their families and other affluent whites who make up most of the readership. We are reminded of how totally one-sided and inhumane is a society ruled by one race of people, and dominated by one class – the moneyed white folk.

We can assume that Miss L. (referred to in several editorials) is Lydia, and the father, deputy and so on are the people on the Whitechapel plantation, or at least people very like them. As with Chapter 6, we see how hard it was for people of humane inclination and dissenting views to be heard. One good white person alone was, and is, not enough. It takes a whole community dedicated to justice for all, if an evil system is to be undone. As if to ironically underline this, we realise that the recommendation of 200 lashes for a runaway slave may well have been what prompted Mr Whitechapel to impose his fatal punishment on Chapel. Society dictates to individuals, even the best.

The period covered by the editorials is from before the whipping through to the six months following it. This enables us at last to place the story in time: the death of Chapel happened in early 1810. Slavery was not abolished in the northern USA until 1865. Tragically, freedom for all people was still two whole generations away, when the (fictional but compelling) story of the novel took place.

CHAPTER TWELVE: GREAT GRANDDAUGHTER

This chapter is narrated by one of Whitechapel's great-granddaughters, the third grandchild of his twelfth daughter, and his youngest great-grandchild.

We learn that Whitechapel bathes the small children, teaching them to wash properly. This great-granddaughter learnt that Whitechapel was captured and brought to America on a slave ship when he was ten. The girl has a dream about Africa, in which she eats some strange food and is recognised by her left-handedness as the great-grandchild of their son. Whitechapel tells her to make her dreams here (in America), not in Africa. He says Africa is his past, not hers. If he choses not to dream about it, she should not dream about it either.

The girl is older than Chapel. She recalls how happy her grandfather was when he married for the second time, but then remembers the change – his 'deadened eyes'– after Chapel's death. She recollects the whipping, giving her version. She recalls Whitechapel informing them of his decision to tell the master where his son was, maintaining that this would ensure his safety. The slaves did not understand the 'special circumstances' Whitechapel claimed would ensure his son's well-being (the fact that Chapel was half white, by Sanders' father). They expected the whipping, and could not understand why Whitechapel was surprised.

After the death of Chapel, the girl stops dreaming of Africa and instead has nightmares about the whipping. The chapter ends with her washing her grandfather after his death.

This chapter gives us a new view of Whitechapel, through the eyes of his great-granddaughter. Through her eyes we see how he was respected by the other slaves, and admired, until the day he 'betrayed' (in their eyes) his son. Because they didn't know the story of the boy's real father, they didn't understand why the old slave believed he could obtain leniency for the boy. They believed that he was crazy, and blamed him for Chapel's death. In the words of his grandchild, 'He shrank in stature before my eyes'. He lost respect and refused to tell anyone the reasoning behind his actions. Finally, the granddaughter feels pity for him once he is ostracised and despised by the other slaves, most of whom are his own children, grandchildren and great-grandchildren. The dissolution of his dignity is somehow summed up by the ritual of bathing. Whitechapel has been reduced to the task of bathing the small children. In the end, after his death, his granddaughter washes him. This reversal of roles, where he has ceased to be the wise grandfather and has become childlike, is a sad reminder of how this once proud and noble man has fallen.

The dream and conversations about Africa reflect modern discussion about black Americans rediscovering their heritage as African-Americans. The debate has raged for a long time about whether they should seek a new identity by harking back to the Africa of their roots, or by resolutely building a place for themselves alongside white Americans

*in their new home. To what extent do African-Americans identify them-
selves as Africans, and to what extent they see themselves as Americans?
It is a thorny question still, to which the text briefly alludes. Modern
Americans, particularly since the black movement and the changes
wrought by black activist Malcolm X, are concerned about the loss of
their African heritage, and trying to re-create links with this heritage.
Whitechapel's answer is clear: Africa was his past, not theirs. The new
generation should make their dreams in America. However, just as this is
a chapter showing how much Whitechapel's views were discredited in the
eyes of the younger generations of slaves, so it is clear that this opinion is
also discredited in their eyes. The sad change in the girl's dreaming is a
reflection of the severing the desire to share her great-grandfather's life.*

CHAPTER THIRTEEN: SANDERS JUNIOR

This chapter is the voice of Sanders Junior, immediately after the death of
Whitechapel. Sanders says he will dig the old man's grave and arrange a
headstone. He admits that he liked the old man, who taught him years
before how to be an overseer. He confesses he shouldn't have hit him on
the day of the whipping, but excuses it because he felt the old man was
undermining his authority by contradicting him in front of the other slaves.
He comments that he didn't use a fist or draw blood, only inflicted a slap.

Sanders saw Chapel as headstrong, questioning, wild, always one
who was likely to run away. He blames Whitechapel for failing to stop the
boy from running away. He says Chapel was given duties at the house to
stop him from escaping, and that Whitechapel was supposed to keep an
eye on him. He speaks of a conversation in which Mr Whitechapel had
said the next runaway would get 200 lashes, as recommended in *The Virginian*. Sanders says that even if he'd known the boy was his half-brother
he 'would have had no choice but to carry out the punishment'. He says
Mr Whitechapel may have reduced the number of lashes, but that the
whipping would have taken place nonetheless.

Sanders covers the dead body of Whitechapel with his jacket, as-
serting that he didn't mean to kill the boy, just to teach him a lesson. He
says he emulated his father, but admits that Whitechapel was a purer and
more courageous man. He admits that he would have liked Whitechapel
as a father.

*This extraordinary chapter presents us with an interior view of the man
most likely to seem the novel's villain: Sanders Junior, the overseer who*

struck Whitechapel and whipped his son to death before his eyes. Instead of being shown as a monster, he is depicted as having human qualities; as having feelings, including insecurity in his own authority over the slaves, ability to like the old man, admitting he was wrong even though it is now too late, and burying the old man in a caring way.

When he makes the dead Whitechapel a farewell gift of his jacket, Sanders demonstrates a quite unexpected fondness for the old slave. It is a clue to the way the white man, too, was locked into his own version of confinement. For Sanders, in his role as overseer, keeping control of the slaves and the appearance of lacking feelings was part of his job, however much he may have privately regretted it. This incident shows us another side, a hint of feelings suppressed – and not the inhuman monster that the whipping made him appear. His astonishing comment breaks yet another barrier: 'If you were white I would have wanted you as my father'. In his heart of hearts, Sanders knows the old black man to have been a far better person than his own white father. It is perhaps the most resonant line in the novel! This chapter shows yet another example of the way the system prevented people from relating to each other in a natural way. Natural feelings and actions were suppressed and the system of authority upheld .

We now understand another aspect of Whitechapel's guilt. The escape was predicted and Whitechapel was given the task of preventing it by constantly watching over the boy. We understand at last his comment in Chapter One about always being the one to go to sleep last and wake first.

EPILOGUE: FORGETTING

Whitechapel imagines what he might have said to Chapel, telling him how to survive as a slave in order to keep him alive. He recognises, however, that Chapel's blood heritage (from Sanders) made him different from the other slaves.

Whitechapel reveals that he knew of his son's dreams about loving Lydia, but thought Chapel realised it was a fantasy which could never be fulfilled. He saw too late that while he sought only survival for his son, Chapel was trying to turn his fantasies into reality.

Whitechapel now reflects that perhaps survival was not the best goal. Better to have a short life under such an inhuman system than to live a long time. He senses the approach of death and welcomes it.

One of the deepest paradoxes for all those who are enslaved or otherwise abused is revisited in this final chapter. Whitechapel says, 'I do not care about your happiness; your life is everything to me'. The old man, unlike his wife and son, placed survival above everything. Yet in the time just before death, he recognises the validity of other priorities.

'Lydia is a part of the dream you tried to make a part of your life. To choose. To have. To keep.' Choice, dreams, independence, self-realisation – these were Chapel's goals, and the old man belatedly acknowledges them. 'I have been wrong all my days,' he says bitterly. His grief is not just personal loss, but a sense of being 'wrong'. We now fully understand why he has given up his white man's name (revealed in the Prologue). Perhaps self-assertion, even rebellion, are right, in their way, however fatal to the individual in the short term. Here is a significant link to the larger political context of the story – including modern day black activism.

He has lived a long time and created for himself a bearable life as a slave. He thought this was the best way. His ambitions for his son, too, were limited to survival. Yet he failed even in this, and his view of himself as guide and protector has been destroyed. Survival at any cost no longer seems the right goal. He himself is a living testimony to that. To survive without freedom, without dignity, without hope, is not worth it. Whitechapel, who put his whole trust in another man's system, has been betrayed. He has been stripped of everything that was important to him. He has nothing left but memories, the bitter memories of an old man who realises the intolerable truth: his whole life he was wrong. His memories, like his life, are now painful, and he welcomes death, as do only those who have given up hope. The old man's embrace of death gives the book a dark, haunting conclusion. It sums up in its hopelessness, the heartbreaking tragedy of the whole system to which it so obviously refers.

CHARACTERS, THEMES AND ISSUES

Characters

The lives of the main characters in this novel are interwoven on several levels. There is the master-slave relationship, but there are other relationships also, from the rape which made Sanders and Chapel half brothers, to the mentor relationship between the old slave, Whitechapel, and the young Sanders. Each of the main characters is developed as fully as possible within the restraints of the narrative structure. As D'Aguiar has said, 'A writer has to portray all characters as complex human beings in order to make those characters' motives and behaviours – however selfish or evil – convincing to readers.' (Interview with the author, cited above.) The following notes offer a brief summary of the key characters, together with suggestions concerning what they represent in the 'argument' of the novel.

WHITECHAPEL: THE GOOD SLAVE

Whitechapel seems on the face of it the hero of the novel. The old slave is regarded by Mr Whitechapel, the plantation owner, as 'noble, honourable, true. He has been tested in ways that could break most men. He is living proof that slaves are our equal in every way'. The other slave owners also see him as 'a slaver's dream'. Even Sanders Junior, the overseer, regards him as a mentor and a likeable old man.

His wife, too, confirms this positive view. She sees him as an example of a slave who did everything in order to survive decently under the system, who did so with dignity, and who used his influence to protect her from harm. She respects his way of life and is grateful to him for saving her when she was raped by Sanders Senior. However, her acquiescence in his views is not complete. She keeps from him the knowledge of their son's secret meetings with Lydia because she knows he will stop it.

As we grasp the true complexity of D'Aguiar's portrait of the old slave, we cannot help but notice the indications that we are not meant to simply admire and agree with Whitechapel. He may be noble and well intentioned, but is his way right? We must take account not only of the dissenting views of his wife and Chapel, but also note the change in Whitechapel. He once saw himself, as Mr Whitechapel sees him, as a 'model slave', 'master of his own slavery'. Now, however, after his failure to save his son from death, he sees himself as a 'killer of children'. His trust in the white man has had disastrous consequences. He is shattered not only by this view of himself, and by his guilt over his son's death, but also by his new understanding about a lifetime's 'ideology' of passivity. His grandchildren come to view him with pity and derision and nickname him 'Sour-face'. And his own despair at himself is correspondingly intense.

The question raised in the novel is whether Whitechapel's response to slavery – being the 'model slave' – is in fact admirable as a way to make slavery bearable, or a co-operation in his own slavery which makes slave-control easier for the plantation owners and overseers.

MR WHITECHAPEL: THE ENLIGHTENED PLANTATION OWNER CAUGHT IN A MORAL QUANDARY

Mr Whitechapel has inherited the plantation from his father. He is a second generation slave-owner who knows no other way of life. The derision of other plantation owners shows the difficulties he faces in trying to be a humane slave-owner. His attempt to show humanity is doomed to failure, we come to see, because it is a contradiction in terms. Compassion and oppression are not compatible.

We see that even under the most decent of slave-owners (like Mr Whitechapel), the lot of the slave is a terrible one: not just lifelong bondage, but constant threats of beating, hard work, lack of medical treatment. Whitechapel describes his master as '...the one person who had the authority to decide whether the day would bring toil, tears or joy to each of us belonging to him simply by snapping his fingers'. There is still, always, the idea of a gap between slave and master, a gulf premised on the idea that slaves are sub-human, not having the feelings or qualities of a white person. While arguing at one point that Whitechapel is proof that slaves are equal to white people in terms of humanness, Mr Whitechapel also argues that slaves are inferior. In trying to balance humanity and slave owning, his views have become an intolerable series of contradictions. This is well recognised by the other plantation owners, who accuse him of hypocrisy.

Despite his view of himself as a good Christian and humane slave-owner, Mr Whitechapel condones the whipping. Sanders comments that Mr Whitechapel may have reduced the number of lashes, or advocated going light with the whip, but he had already decided that an example was to be made of the next runaway. Sanders Senior tells a story of a previous whipping of a runaway who later died, observed by the previous Mr Whitechapel and his two sons, one of whom was 'grey' and one 'more stalwart'. We are not told which was which, but clearly the experience did not affect the present Mr Whitechapel enough to prevent him from ordering the same punishment again. While D'Aguiar avoids stereotyping characters like this, there can be little doubt that Mr Whitechapel represents the system. He may not be evil by nature, but he collaborates in an evil, however reluctantly. We should beware against exonerating him because he is a 'nice man'. Many evil systems have been sustained by unthinking individuals, whose charm cannot disguise in the long run their complicity in evil.

CHAPEL: THE RUNAWAY
AND REBEL AGAINST SLAVERY

Chapel is young, idealistic, with dreams of making a living from poetry if he reaches the north. He dreams of his children being born free. Having tasted the forbidden fruit of reading and writing, he longs for a life of freedom and dreams of loving Lydia.

Half-black, half-white, Chapel doesn't fit the image of Whitechapel's son, the model slave. He wants to turn his dreams into reality, and, after the death of his mother, he takes the risk of running away without fully realising the consequences. There is a sense in which Chapel's death is a result of simply giving up. Betrayed, he thinks, by his adopted father, with no hope of ever being a free man with the girl he loves. With his beloved mother already dead, he welcomes his own death. The 'spiritual death' he has already suffered precipitates his physical death.

His short and tragic life, full of promise and extinguished so brutally, demonstrates clearly the crushing effects of slavery on a bright young boy for whom life, under other circumstances, could have been full of joy.

SANDERS: THE OVERSEER

Sanders Junior is portrayed early in the novel as the cruel overseer who whips Chapel to death. However, when he is finally allowed a voice (Chapter 13), we see in him a more complex personality, not merely a bad character.

We discover that young Sanders grew up with his widowed father who was grieving over his mother's death in childbirth. The boy spent time following Whitechapel around while he was growing up. His father remarried – a loveless marriage – and spent as much time as possible working. Sanders Senior viewed slaves as sub-human and in need of being beaten.

Young Sanders adopted his father's attitude to slaves, while at the same time liking Whitechapel, the mentor of his childhood and youth, whom he admits, at the end of the novel, he would have liked as a father 'if he had been white'. We see in him the contradictions at the heart of the system: an unconscious absorption of attitudes to slaves as inferior and of slave management through beating, while there is another side which could have allowed him to befriend a slave if it had not been for their relative positions.

Themes

SLAVERY: SYSTEMATIC OPPRESSION

Slavery is the main theme of *The Longest Memory*. However, because the novel has a lot to say about slavery, it is sensible to break this theme into sub-themes dealing with issues about particular aspects of slavery.

THE HORRORS OF SLAVERY

We cannot miss the central point of *The Longest Memory*: slavery was a monstrous system, by definition a human tragedy. If we think about the novel's structure, we realise that it circles repeatedly round three incidents: the rapes (of cook), the whippings (of the unnamed slave in Chapter 3 and twice, of Chapel), and the grievous mistake of Whitechapel when he handed in his son. All of them tell us of the savagery of the system. A white man could take advantage of a black woman, just because he felt like it. A black slave could be beaten for reading, and whipped to death for trying to escape. An old man, trying to save his son, could trust to a lifetime's faithful service, and be let down by his masters without a moment's consideration. Although it does not attempt a broad historical survey, the novel nonetheless shows us in the specific horrors of one man's family the bestiality of a whole system.

'I have buried two wives and most of my children,' Whitechapel says. The life of a slave was unpredictable. Combinations of ill-treatment, poor diet, hard work and lack of medical treatment led to a much higher death rate than among the white population. Even Whitechapel, though he was given time off work to take care of his wife, was unable to persuade Mr Whitechapel to pay for a doctor to come when she was dying of fever. Even the more humane slave owners did not provide medical treatment for slaves. Sick slaves recovered or died without medicine. Most of Whitechapel's children also died without reaching old age. It is noticeable that whereas Whitechapel accepts the master's view that his wife's time has come, he does not accept the brutal death of his son.

The mistreatment was not just physical, of course. Loss of dignity, loss of hope, even emotional trauma were part of the tragedy. The loss of family is is an important theme in black American (and Australian) literature. Slavery (and racist policies here) caused the breaking up of families as well as early deaths for many. One of the editorials in Chapter 11 takes as its subject the separation of a slave woman and her children through a sale. The attitude taken, which we can assume was the prevalent view of the times, is that slaves are not truly human and do not have the same feelings as white people. The mother's feelings are likened to the attachment of a cow to its calf, not to human love. The slaves are referred to as an 'investment' from which the best return should be obtained, 'even if it means breaking up the capital into smaller holdings and selling each holding separately'. The callousness of this treatment of human beings, and the enormity of calmly advocating the splitting of a family in terms of capital and return on investment is stunning in its cruelty. From a contemporary viewpoint, it is hard to imagine the rhetoric being believed, yet we know it was believed at the time. The treatment of people as things, which was institutionalised in slavery, must wreck havoc, and *The Longest Memory* shows us the grief it could produce.

Loss and grief are a strong theme in black American literature. In this novel the effect of loss, on top of a lifetime of injustice, is dramatised searingly in the living death suffered by Whitechapel after Chapel dies. His life thereafter holds no joy. Undertones of loss and grief appear throughout the whole story, but they focus on the despair of Whitechapel, without any doubt the central character. As we know the outcome, even in the happier scenes are pervaded by a sense of impending doom. And, as suggested above, the heartbreak of one man, a good man who tried his very best to live with the system, sums up a whole evil regime.

RESPONSES TO OPPRESSION: TWO KINDS OF SLAVES

Whitechapel views slavery as inescapable and best survived by a combination of obedience, hard work, dignity and respect for the master. He believes that the model slave will then be treated with civility and fairness. These views are born out of his experience over many years as a slave, and he sees it as a bearable way of life.

Chapel, however, sees slavery as a jail, restricting his freedom, forbidding him to read, preventing his life from taking its natural course. He finds it difficult to accept the life of a slave.

Whitechapel argues that there are two kinds of slaves. The first kind is the compliant, respectful, submissive slave who observes and avoids the mistakes made by others. The second kind is rebellious and learns only by making mistakes and being punished for them.

These two responses to slavery are contrasted in the characters of Whitechapel and Chapel. It was D'Aguiar's intention to show two ways of responding to oppression, both of them understandable, though incompatible.

> Whitechapel [had had]...a reasonable life...because he lived without hurting others. He tried to minimise his pain and maximise his respect and dignity and I think that is a fair end to his life, given his circumstances....I wanted him to be solid to show a world that it paid to be unchanging and in the middle of that world to have a young person coming along and saying I am sorry to hear what you are saying but – no way. (Interview with the author, cited above).

It is clear that Whitechapel's way ensures survival and avoids the whip, but ultimately it is also the way the institution of slavery is upheld. Slaves like Whitechapel enable the system to continue, which is why there is considerable irony in the other slave owners wanting to buy him. By ensuring his own personal survival and the smooth running of his life within an inhumane system, Whitechapel also contributes to the smooth running of the plantation and the slave system. He is the model slave, the compliant 'Uncle Tom' who keeps the other slaves on the plantation in order, following his lead. He teaches his children and grandchildren to be good slaves. He is valued, not for himself, but for his role in showing how a good slave should live.

Chapel, on the other hand, is rebellious, troublesome, questioning, dreaming of a better life. Although he brings about his own suffering, he is standing up for something worthwhile. The reason why runaways are punished so harshly is because escape undermines the system, inciting other slaves to also dream of freedom.

Chapel's rebellion is set in the era of slavery, but his righteous rebellion against the advice of a cautious parent is a universal theme. Most teenagers rebel at some time with the confidence of youth against the advice of parents who are concerned about protecting and keeping them safe. Safety is not a high priority of youth, while adventure and experience are. Seen in this context, Chapel's natural rebellion against his father's wise but cautious advice becomes, under slavery, a crime punishable by death. It is yet another instance of the system rendering natural relationships impossible.

MANAGEMENT OF SLAVES: TWO KINDS OF MASTER

Just as there are two views amongst the slaves, there are also two contrasting views held by the slave owners about how slaves should be managed.

Mr Whitechapel represents the humane slave owner. He provides reasonable living conditions and food and does not permit gratuitous cruelty on his plantation. Sanders Senior and the other plantation owners represent the view that slaves are merely property, like cattle and other stock, and should be beaten into submission. The conversation between Mr Whitechapel and the other owners at the Club demonstrates the differences between their views. However, what is most noticeable is that the outcome, whipping a slave to death, is the same. Both kinds of owners regard slaves as less human than themselves, and both are unconcerned about the slaves as people. Even humane slave management is to a significant extent a strategy to ensure compliance, with obedient slaves being the aim of all plantation owners.

Incipient rebellion is always present when people are in a situation where one group of people is controlled by another. Wherever one group is oppressed by a smaller but powerful authority group (dictatorships, jails etc) there is a constant threat of rebellion by the oppressed masses. To avoid rebellion, the overseers and owners had to seem all-powerful, so that rebellion would not seem worth the risk, be seen as doomed to fail. The power and powerlessness had to be constantly reinforced in a situation where a large slave population (some three million) was controlled by a handful of plantation owners and overseers.

There are repeated comments by Mr Whitechapel, Sanders and others which suggest that slaves are different from white people, not equal, less intelligent, and so on. Such comments today are recognised as racist and based on prejudice, but in the nineteenth century such beliefs were widely held even by those who regarded themselves as reasonable and humane people. Sanders Senior went so far as to claim that any ambiguity would be interpreted by the slaves as a sign of weakness. It was therefore essential to appear to be in control at all times and to reinforce control.

Ownership of slaves made them the property of the plantation owners. They belonged to the owner just like the stock and other inanimate property. 'Your lives aren't yours, but his,' Sanders Junior comments. In the end, humane and cruel masters have the same goal – control of the slaves – which is incompatible with kindness, as we see in the case of Mr Whitechapel's failure to prevent a slave being whipped to death.

The problem caused by the runaway is not the loss of a slave, but the fear that the other slaves will become restless and dissatisfied, and so the whole plantation system will collapse. The capture and punishment of a runaway is therefore intended as a lesson to the other slaves that attempting to escape is too dangerous. However, by whipping the boy to death, Sanders created a disturbing mood of rebellion among the remaining slaves, raising fears of a revolt.

Sanders Senior tells his son that 'slaves are different in intelligence and human standing before God'. He also reveals his fear of mass revolt, posing the question the slave owners and overseers all shared 'What if they turned against us all?' His attitudes contain none of the ambiguity expressed by Mr Whitechapel, an ambiguity which Sanders teaches his son not to show.

Lydia, however, represents the next generation, as does Chapel. Initially, the strangeness of these different cultures allows the myth of inferiority to be perpetuated, but as children grow up together they come to recognise that essentially there is no difference in the human qualities of blacks and whites. Through several generations of living together, the myth of inequality, which formed the basis on which slavery could be justified, could not be sustained.

Fraternisation with slaves was discouraged and derided, yet it was impossible to prevent when living in such close proximity. The case of Sanders Senior and the cook, and of Lydia and Chapel, while very different, are examples of the impossibility of trying to keep the two groups of people separate. Mr Whitechapel comments on the single thread which, over generations, has woven itself into 'a prodigious carpet'. This is almost inevitable where families live in close proximity over several generations, and as time goes on the fallacy that the slaves are inferior humans becomes harder and harder to sustain.

SLAVERY AND CHRISTIANITY

Mr Whitechapel sees himself as a Christian and a slave-owner. Like other plantation owners, he does not see this as a contradiction in terms. He believes in humane treatment of slaves, but he also believes in slavery. He says 'I promote the teachings of Christ and practise slavery'. The other slave-owners also regard themselves as Christians. Saying 'Christianity does not equal weakness,' enables them to excuse brutality towards slaves without seeing any contradiction. So, too, they argue that God is for whites, not for the slaves.

This issue is discussed in one of the editorials (Chapter 11), which seeks to separate the two by saying that Christianity is a faith and has nothing to do with slavery, which is an economic institution. The editorial argues that one can treat a slave with Christian fairness and instruct him in Christian beliefs, without arguing that he is our equal before God. What is clear, however, is that if the African is seen as equal, then there can be no moral justification for slavery. The editor admits, 'Once we extend Christian values to include slaves we then throw into question the very basis of our forced enslavement of them'.

It is therefore essential for these Christian slave-owners to continually prove that slaves are not equals, in order to justify slavery. Clearly, they have difficulty maintaining their belief in the inequality of the races, yet they manage this self-deception because it sustains their defence of slavery, which is seen by them as essential to the economic running of big plantations. Any hint that slaves might see themselves as equal to white people is a threat, and the response is anger and harsh punishment.

This is the background to the seemingly hypocritical prayer of Mr Whitechapel and Sanders following the whipping to death of a slave. The man has just killed his brother, and they pray, not for forgiveness, but for God's guidance in dealing with slaves. So too, Sanders Senior can rape a slave woman while still maintaining he is a Christian, of higher 'intelligence and human standing before God' than the slaves. The contradiction so apparent to us is not at all apparent to them. The views shown to us in the novel were common of the nineteenth century. The contradictions were not obvious, and the view of superior and inferior races was not seriously questioned. God was the God of the white races, or as one of the plantation owners says 'God is for us, not them'.

If nothing else, this enables us to see how far we have come, but also how far humans can deceive themselves and maintain attitudes in perfect sincerity which have no real foundation.

MEMORY AND FORGETTING:
THE PARADOX OF HISTORY

The novel's title refers in the most obvious sense to Whitechapel's age. He has outlived most of his contemporaries and his children. He is a very old man when the novel opens and his memory goes back further than that of anyone else on the plantation, including the owner and the overseer. Whitechapel's long memory is not merely an interesting fact in the novel, it is an integral part of the story and points to a major theme.

What does Whitechapel remember? Pain – the pain of a life of slavery. 'Memory hurts,' he says, with awful simplicity. The rape of his wife and the brutal death by whipping of his adopted son are key memories, but the other insults and savageries of the system are part of what is implicitly referred to. And because he remembers, the injustice lives on. For example, once everyone else was dead, the sorry story of Sanders' father raping a slave woman could have been forgotten, buried in the past, except for the living memory of Whitechapel. The white sons of the owner and overseer step into their fathers' positions, but the past, in the form of Whitechapel, who knows and remembers, still haunts them. The old man dies in mortal pain. It is not physical, but spiritual. The past lives on in him until he can bear the pain no longer.

There is also a sense in which *The Longest Memory* refers to the collective memory of a race of people forced into slavery. Every individual, each personal story that is remembered and retained, adds to the collective memory of black American history. Whitechapel's memories are important to his people. His is not just an individual story, but one example of the story of his people. There were, we know, many Whitechapels and Chapels, whose individual stories were profoundly sad like those of the characters in this novel. Collectively, they are an indictment of the evils of slavery and a record of a terrible history of oppression.

The novel begins with 'Remembering' and ends with 'Forgetting'. These sections of the novel deal with another aspect of this theme which is often found in black American literature: the contradictory impulses to suppress the past or confront it. Like Whitechapel, many chose to suppress memory because it is too painful to remember. So in the first section, 'Remembering', we witness the memory hurting so much that it caused physical pain. By the last section, 'Forgetting', Whitechapel is confronting the memory, trying to come to terms with his past. He is imagining what he would say to Chapel. He is confronting his feeling of having failed as a father, his guilt, his mistakes, the understanding which enabled him to survive, but which proved to be wrong and was unable to prevent the death of Chapel. The message of 'Remembering' is 'Memory hurts...I forget as hard as I can'. The concluding line of 'Forgetting' is 'Forget. Memory is pain trying to resurrect itself'. Thus the book moves in a circle from remembering (what is so important) to forgetting (what is too painful to bear) in a cycle that we realise is much the same as the experience of African Americans as a whole. In a paradoxical way, the book seems to argue for both remembering and forgetting. Let us not hide the terrible things of the past, for they must be faced. Let us also forget, and get on with life now.

IDENTITY AND SELF-ESTEEM

Names, or lack of them, are significant in establishing the way people in this novel feel about themselves. What they are called, and how they see their names, tells us a lot about the identity crises they face.

On the first page, we hear Whitechapel deciding that henceforth he will have no name. He rejects the name he has used all these years, the name of his master, bestowed on him when he was brought from Africa. Along with the name, he rejects his identity as Whitechapel, the good and obedient slave, who has some influence with the master and can expect in return some consideration and sympathy. The killing of the boy demonstrated to Whitechapel the errors of his view of himself, as he was made forcefully aware that he was only a slave, not entitled to any special privileges or consideration, or even to treatment as a human like other humans. By rejecting his name, he rejects the self who turned in his son, believing it was in the boy's best interests and believing in his own power to obtain leniency. He also rejects his association with the master through the sharing of his name, an association which made him put loyalty to his master before unity with the other slaves. In many ways, prior to the whipping, he was closer to the master than to the other slaves, a kind of right-hand man, faithful employee, trusted assistant or 'Uncle Tom'. The whipping of his son and the scorn heaped on him demonstrated how wrong he had been. In fact, he was only a slave, a person of small value and not deserving of any special consideration or respect. This realisation caused him to reject the name Whitechapel and all it represented. Nothing he did, though, was able to bridge the gap between himself and the other slaves who blamed him for the boy's death. He was neither one of them, nor part of the establishment. He was entirely alone, without respect from masters or slaves.

Whitechapel had passed on his name to the boy, son of his wife and Sanders Senior. Whitechapel had married the woman and raised the boy as his son, giving him his name. However, the woman never called her son Whitechapel, shortening the name instead to Chapel. She says this was because two Whitechapels would have been confusing, but we suspect that it is also because she is conscious that the boy is not Whitechapel's son. Nor, to pick up a more subtler hint, was he like his adopted father. The different name emphasises his difference from both Whitechapel the slave and Whitechapel the master.

The key elements of the name, 'white' and 'chapel', have specific connotations (discussed in the 'Points to note'). Among other things, they suggest the use of white Christianity to give some moral credibility to and to disguise the patent immorality of slavery. By bestowing his name on his slave, the first Mr Whitechapel reinforced the slave's identification with the interests of the master.

It is also noticeable that unlike the other characters, the cook, Whitechapel's second wife and Chapel's mother, remains nameless. Her story is told, but it is peripheral to the issues raised in the novel. The rape is not in itself the main story. It features in the novel to show the brutality of Sanders Senior, the decency of Mr Whitechapel, and the love and humanity of Whitechapel the slave. The cook is slave, victim, wife, and mother. She has a series of roles in relation to other people, and despite her pivotal role in the lives of the men who are the major characters, she is not a major character. Her name therefore is unimportant. Her lack of a name also recalls the use of the same device in two seminal works of black literature: *The Invisible Man*, by black American writer Ralph Ellison, and *Wild Cat Falling*, by indigenous Australian Mudrooroo. In both novels, incredibly, the central characters are nameless. It argues a profound identity crisis, linked to their being caught between black culture and a white society.

Identity, or lack of it, was a significant factor in the lives of the slaves, but also for Mr Whitechapel, the plantation owner. He, too, is conscious of his name and of the legacy from his father. After the whipping, he doesn't think he deserves the name Whitechapel, yet he goes to the Club where he meets with the other plantation owners and he identifies himself as one of them, although he disagrees with their view of slaves as less than human. The other owners call his ideas about slaves mad and dangerous. Ironically, it is Whitechapel's actions as the model slave which makes the other slave owners accept his views. Through Whitechapel's sacrifice, Mr Whitechapel's way of treating slaves is vindicated and he is accepted by the other owners. He concludes 'At last, I am without shame. My name is restored to me'.

Learning to write the name Whitechapel is a significant part of Chapel's education. Lydia first teaches him to read, then to write his name, which is also her name. However, the incident serves to emphasise for the reader the disparity between the two children. Though both share the name, one is a plantation owner's daughter while the other is a slave. For one, the name is a proud heritage, while for the other it is merely a mark of ownership.

CHOICE, RESPONSIBILITY AND FATE

Each character in the novel makes deliberate choices, and these choices determine the final outcome. Many of these choices are ultimately fatal ones in the larger picture, though in most instances the motives of those concerned were good ones. The only outright 'bad' choice was that of Sanders Senior, deciding to give in to lust, and twice rape the slave woman, Chapel's mother. All the others believed they were doing 'good'. But in an unjust world, even 'good' choices can have bad consequences.

Lydia chooses to teach Chapel to read and write. Her motives are innocent and idealistic. She is a child and it is natural for her to pass on knowledge to a younger child. Nevertheless, she knows it is forbidden for slaves to learn to read and write. Her choice gives Chapel hopes and dreams which he otherwise might not have had.

Chapel's mother knows about his reading with Lydia, but her pride in his achievement is stronger than her fear about it being forbidden. She chooses not to notice. Later, she takes the message to Lydia which brings about the secret meetings between Lydia and Chapel. Again, the mother chooses to support love rather than advising caution. She also chooses not to tell Whitechapel, because she knows he will prevent it.

The combination of learning to read, the encouragement of Lydia's love, and his own dreams of freedom bring about Chapel's decision to run away. He rejects his father's advice, refuses to make the best of his life as a slave, and makes the choice, with Lydia's support, to run away to the north to freedom. This action leads, almost inevitably, to death.

Running away is Chapel's choice, but having him brought back when he might have escaped is Whitechapel's choice. Thinking it is for the best, Whitechapel tells the master where he is. Mr Whitechapel, in turn, chooses to leave the plantation, and this leaves a fatal gap into which Sanders steps.

The final fatal choice is made by Sanders Junior, who in the absence of Mr Whitechapel decides to administer 200 lashes to the boy he doesn't know is his half brother. It is ironic that his choice of 200 lashes was based on a newspaper editorial which opposed killing runaway slaves, but argued that 200 lashes was 'just and fair' as punishment intended to warn against others running away.

While Whitechapel blames himself for the choice which led to his son's recapture and death, we as readers can see that the tragedy was the outcome of a series of inextricable choices made by various people which impacted on one another, resulting finally in tragedy.

BETRAYAL

B etrayals are abound in this novel. Like the fatal choices (above), they are largely unintentional. The exception is Sanders Senior raping his slave cook before and after her marriage to Whitechapel, betraying Mr Whitechapel's trust in him to treat the slaves with humanity and not to abuse them.

Most obvious is Whitechapel's betrayal of his son, which results in the boy's death and leaves the father shattered by guilt, shame, and the destruction of his view of the world. The old slave told his master where his son could be found, trusting that his own position and their shared private knowledge of the boy's parentage would ensure his safety and a suitable, but not cruel, punishment – preferable to the boy's death at the hands of strangers. Mr Whitechapel's betrayal of this trust was unintentional. He did not plan to have the boy whipped to death, but his absence, the overseer's anger, and the deputy's failure to carry out instructions led to an absolute betrayal of Whitechapel's trust.

Perhaps the most poignant of all is Lydia's unintentional betrayal. By teaching Chapel to read and write, meeting him at night, feeding his dreams and persuading him to run away, Lydia inadvertently pushed him towards death. Just as when she taught him the forbidden skills of reading and writing, it was Lydia who led the way, but Chapel who took the risk and the punishment, so too when she persuaded him to run away she ran no risk herself. She was absent when he was beaten for reading, and absent again when he was whipped for running away.

Chapel's mother, too, aided the runaway and betrayed her husband by concealing firstly the reading and secondly the secret meetings with Lydia. By keeping these things from her husband, she prevented him from doing anything to stop Chapel before it was too late. Whitechapel believed the boy's dreams about Lydia were mere fantasies, because he did not know that they are actually already meeting secretly at night.

While the tragic chain of events began with the deliberate betrayal of trust by Sanders Senior, it was the series of well-meaning betrayals which resulted in the boy's death. In the end, the system which decreed death as the punishment for a runaway slave proved to be stronger than the good intentions of Whitechapel, Lydia and Mr Whitechapel.

LOVE

Love is a universal theme of literature. In *The Longest Memory,* various different kinds of love are explored. Though the book has a tragic outcome, it can be argued that its treatment of love offers a counterpoint to the otherwise brutal and cheerless world it depicts.

The paternal love of Whitechapel for the boy who was like a son to him is arguably the strongest, shining brightly and purely throughout the novel, stronger even than his feelings of failure and guilt. It is a pure, unsullied, generous kind of love, which seeks only to protect the boy from harm.

In contrast, Lydia's love for Chapel is a romantic love, fed by dreams and fantasies, based partly on sexual desire, but also on a meeting of minds and a desire to form a family. It is an innocent love, and beautiful, even if in the end it leads to the tragedy which the father is trying to prevent.

> I wanted love to be there, I wanted love across races to be there, to show
> that these barriers are established but that it is possible to break them, and
> that love actually knows no boundary. (Interview with the author, cited
> above)

D'Aguiar has said that he saw the love between Lydia and Chapel as a high point in the novel, despite its fatal end, an antidote to the gloom all around.

In contrast to these two pure loves is the travesty of 'love' – the rape of Whitechapel's wife by Sanders Senior. This is the epitome of loveless relationships, involving sex by force with to gratify a purely physical need. The woman, regarded as scarcely human is exploited by Sanders Senior and his position of power.

WHAT DO THE CRITICS SAY?

'The skill of the poet D'Aguiar is evident in the brevity of language, cryptic phrases, and powerful images which are at once poetic and painful...The Longest Memory is a remarkable effort by a provocative new voice...' (Brooke Stephens, *Quarterly Black Review*)

'Moving...unique...satisfying. D'Aguiar's writing is graceful and captivating.' (*Los Angeles Times Book Review*)

WHAT THE CRITICS SAY

'Luminous...D'Aguiar brings a subtle but powerful voice to a work that enlarges our customary perceptions of masters and slaves.' (*New York Times Book Review*)

'A fiercely lyrical fiction debut. Explores the conflict among African-American slaves between obedient, stoic survivalists and defiant rebels, adding resonance to his haunting tale.' (*Publishers Weekly*)

'[*The Longest Memory*]...portrays the wide range of psychological and emotional conflicts shared by masters and slaves during the era of American slavery.... [It is] a moving, sensitive tale of black-white relationships affected by blood ties and societal placement, revealing the slave system's complicated bonds and ironic associations...reveals the irreconcilable patterns of thought that build barriers between individuals. The reader discerns how the tragedy that began during slavery continues to produce consequences for today's black and white Americans.' (*Choice*)

'The separate testimonies unravel, in all its tragic poignancy, a story of inter-racial rape in one generation balanced by doomed inter-racial love in the next...This deceptively simple book resonates long after it is finished; it addresses not only the dilemmas of the past but also today's generation gap in racial attitudes.' (*New Statesman and Society*)

'Gripping...The novel earns its heartbreak by its density of moral thought...A brilliant-and beautiful-achievement.'(*The London Independent*)

'Affecting...compelling...D'Aguiar brings a poet's cadence and grace to his work...His story reminds readers, powerfully, why words matter.' (*Virginian Pilot and Ledger-Star*)

'A tender and intense study of the corrosive powers of enchainment...subtly explores how an inhuman system can shackle both captors and captives. Already established as a poet, D'Aguiar marks his accomplished arrival as novelist with this compelling and compassionate work.' (*The London Times*)

SAMPLE ESSAY

The Longest Memory explores how an inhuman system can shackle both captors and captives.

Discuss.

The Longest Memory demonstrates the many ways in which the brutal system of slavery, the institutional oppression of one group of people by another, constrains behaviour and relationships between people. Both the slaves who are the system's victims, and the owners and overseers who are its sustaining authorities, are constrained by the system. Set on a plantation in the southern state of Virginia in the late eighteenth and early nineteenth centuries, Fred D'Aguiar's novel explores the way such a system brings about cruelty and injustice, despite the best intentions of the individuals involved.

Slavery most obviously binds the slaves. They are owned by a white master and regarded as stock rather than people. They are physically confined to the plantation and their lives are regulated by the overseer in terms of work, food, and sleeping times. They are dependent on the master for permission to marry and for their families being kept together. It is easy and acceptable to sell members of a slave family separately in order to make more money from the sale, and indeed fear of losing family members is a major factor which keeps the slaves under control. Chapel, for instance, does not run away while his mother is alive. Another factor is the law against literacy, which prevents slaves from communicating with the outside world. The system of punishments for disobedience and rewards for compliance functions to produce slaves like Whitechapel, who learn to reap the rewards rather than the punishments.

While it is clear that slaves are bound in almost every respect under slavery, The Longest Memory also demonstrates the way plantation owners are shackled by the system. Mr Whitechapel's dilemma as a slave-owner who sees himself as humane and a good Christian is how to keep control of his slaves without abusing them. It is clear that he does try. We are not looking at a heartless owner, but at a man trying to do his best within the system. Nonetheless, despite his best efforts, and those of his father before him, barbarities happen. The cook is raped by the overseer, and the boy, Chapel, is whipped to death before his father's eyes. The other owners regard Mr Whitechapel with derision, mocking his words about humanity and kindness as hypocritical. Yet we cannot simply label him a hypocrite, because he genuinely believes in kindness towards his slaves. *They are well fed and the overseer has strict instructions not to abuse them. Ultimately, it is the inhumanity of the system that requires a small group of people to oppress and control a much larger group which is to blame for the death of Chapel. No-one, not even the overseer Sanders, who orders the whipping, wishes to see the boy die. Yet, in a context of oppression, brutality seems unavoidable and it surely leads to such fatal developments.*

The inhuman system of slavery crushes the natural relationships between people, both captors and captives. The love between Chapel the slave and Lydia the plantation owner's daughter is doomed from the beginning, no matter how genuine their feelings and how passionate their hopes. So too, the mentor relationship between the old slave, Whitechapel, and the young Sanders, cannot be sustained once Sanders becomes overseer and must assert his control. He is unable to show any kindness now, because he must be seen to be in authority. We are poignantly reminded of this when he covers the old man with his jacket after his death, commenting that he could not have done so while the old man was alive. Also, the natural parent-child relationship between Whitechapel and Chapel is twisted by the system. The natural wish of the father to protect becomes a jailer's role, while the natural rebellion of a young man shrugging off his father's wise but cautious advice is punished by death. The relationship between the half brothers, Sanders and Chapel, is kept secret and replaced by the relationship of overseer and slave. The final shocking result is that brother whips brother to death.

The Longest Memory moovingly explores the way natural human behaviour and relationships between people are twisted by the institution of slavery. As long as the slave system exists, it is impossible for the people involved to relate to one another in natural ways. The characters in this novel are shown not as stereotyped villains and victims, but as complex, basically well-meaning individuals. Yet the oppression continues. Based on a presumption of racial inequality, the system which maintains that one race must serve another creates codes of behaviour and social attitudes which cannot avoid destroying people. Certainly it is the captive slaves who suffer most, and whose memories of injustice the novel dramatises. But even the captors cannot escape being depressed. There are no true winners in slavery, only losers, and subsequent generations of pain.